# Little Jesus, Born for Me

The story of Jesus' birth for kids, based on Matthew 1:18-25;
Luke 1:26-35; Luke 2; and John 8:12

Written by Naomi Moon

Illustrated by Eric Freeberg

CONCORDIA PUBLISHING HOUSE · SAINT LOUIS

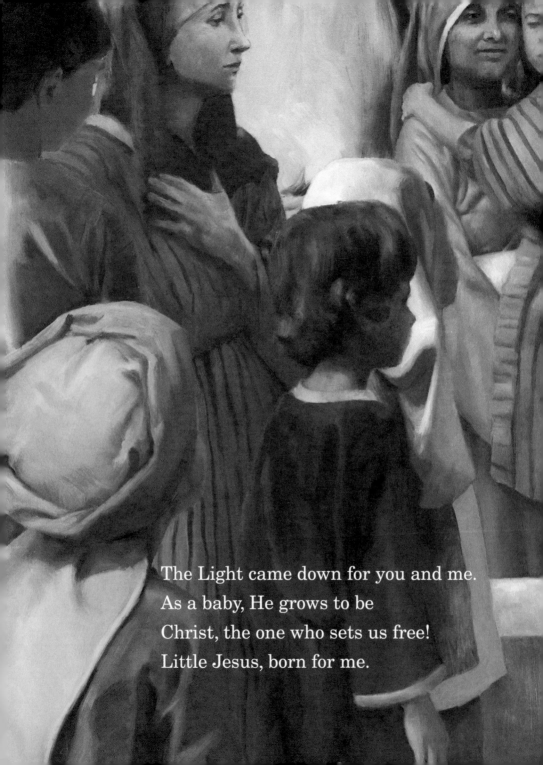

The Light came down for you and me.
As a baby, He grows to be
Christ, the one who sets us free!
Little Jesus, born for me.

Gabriel called overhead:
"Do not be afraid," he said.
"Dear Mary, this Light will spread."
Little Jesus, born for me.

"Joseph, you will love her so,
Make her your wife." Then they go
To Bethlehem, where God would show
Little Jesus, born for me.

Calm and quiet in the night,
Snuggled in and bundled tight,
Son of God came as the Light,
Little Jesus, born for me.

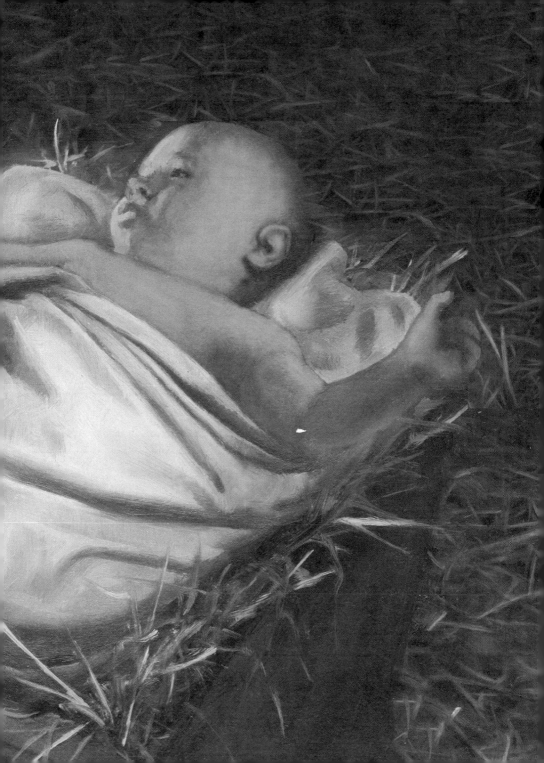

Shepherds followed, in awe of
Angel song so high above,
Leading to the One beloved.
Little Jesus, born for me.

In the manger, see and hear
The Light so there will be no fear.
Good News of great joy, so dear.
Little Jesus, born for me.

Little Savior, born to die.
And in a tomb, He would lie,
Then to rise and reign on high!
Little Jesus, born for me.

The darkness shall be no more.
This Light will last forevermore!
He will come back to restore.
Little Jesus, born for me.